HOPE - THE ANCHOR OF THE SOUL

HOPE - THE ANCHOR OF THE SOUL

Robert Plant & Amanda Le Bail

RITCHIE

John Ritchie Publishing

40 Beansburn, Kilmarnock, Scotland

ISBN-13: 978 1 912522 56 9

Copyright © 2019 by John Ritchie Ltd.
40 Beansburn, Kilmarnock, Scotland

www.ritchiechristianmedia.co.uk

Typeset by John Ritchie Ltd., Kilmarnock
Printed by Bell & Bain Ltd., Glasgow

CONTENTS

Troubles almost 'whelm the soul;
Griefs like billows o'er me roll;
Tempters seek to lure astray;
Storms obscure the light of day:
But in Christ I can be bold,
I've an anchor that shall hold.

William Clark Martin 1864 - 1914

HOPE – THE ANCHOR OF THE SOUL

This is a little book of hope. It is written with the sole intention of helping to ease the pain often caused by sickness, sorrow, disease or death. Several similar books have been written in the past using just selected Bible verses. This one is different as it also adds hymns and verses of poetry to provide a little extra help, comfort and strength to the weary soul.

It is the prayer of the writers that as you read the pages you will discover that despite the apparent storm that you are passing through there is great hope available to those reaching out for it. The Lord Jesus said one day, "Search the scriptures; for in them ye think ye have eternal life: and they are they which testify of me." (John Ch5 v39).

The whole revelation of the Bible is provided to bear witness to the Lord Jesus Christ, the Son of God, as the only hope of salvation and readiness for Heaven. He alone can soothe the aching heart, ease the troubled conscience, dry the weeping eye and cleanse the sinful soul. As you daily read the pages of this book may you find that God is not just the "God of all comfort" (2nd Corinthians Ch1 v3) but the "God of hope" (Romans Ch15 v13) and the "God of salvation" (Psalm 68 v20).

HOPE

*H*ope is a gift that is given,
To those who on life's stormy seas,
All battered by waves, and wind driven -
It gives to the weary soul ease.

*O*ur Anchor we have is in Jesus -
The Answer to all life does send.
Our faith reaches to Him to save us
And steady our paths to the end.

*P*recious - the Words He has spoken,
Founding our faith in their power.
And sure is His promise unbroken
To be with us each day, and each hour.

*E*ven if doubts are assailing
And trials may come, as they do!
Our Anchor will keep us from failing,
And shelter us all the way through.

AleB

Day 1

He maketh the storm a calm,
so that the waves thereof are still.
Psalm 107 v29

For Thou hast been a strength to the poor,
a strength to the needy in his distress,
a refuge from the storm, a shadow from the heat.
Isaiah Ch25 v4

And He (The Lord Jesus) arose and rebuked the wind,
and said unto the sea, Peace, be still.
And the wind ceased, and there was a great calm.
Mark Ch4 v39

We have peace with God
through our Lord Jesus Christ.
Romans Ch5 v1

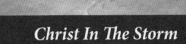

Galilee's waters are raging, on them a vessel is tossed;
Seamen in terror are calling, 'Carest Thou not, we are lost?'
Sweetly asleep on a pillow, Maker and Saviour He lay;
Wild with dismay they awake Him, 'Master, we perish', they say.

Wonderful Jesus, I need Thee, out in the storm and the strife,
Oft it has seemed I was sinking tossed on the ocean of life;
Speak to the winds and the waters, each Thy behest must fulfil;
Speak to my heart in the tempest, whispering softly, 'Be still'.

When I am toiling in rowing, almost engulfed in the sea,
Make of the billows a pathway, come thro' the darkness to me;
Failures and terrors will vanish, soon as I know Thou art nigh;
Say to my soul in the danger, 'Be not afraid, it is I'.

Manie Payne Ferguson. (1850 - 1932)

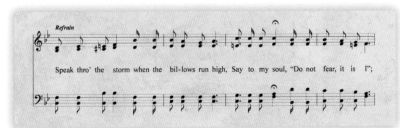

Day 2

The LORD is my shepherd; I shall not want.
He maketh me to lie down in green pastures:
he leadeth me beside the still waters.
He restoreth my soul: he leadeth me
in the paths of righteousness for his name's sake.
Yea, though I walk through the valley
of the shadow of death,
I will fear no evil: for thou art with me;
thy rod and thy staff they comfort me.
Thou preparest a table before me
in the presence of mine enemies:
thou anointest my head with oil; my cup runneth over.
Surely goodness and mercy
shall follow me all the days of my life:
and I will dwell in the house of the LORD for ever.
Psalm 23

Then said Jesus unto them ...
Verily, verily, I say unto you, I am the door of the sheep.
I am the good shepherd:
the good shepherd giveth his life for the sheep.
I am the good shepherd, and know my sheep,
and am known of mine.
John Ch10 v7, 11-14

Jesus my Shepherd is,
'Twas He that loved my soul,
'Twas He that cleansed me by His blood,
'Twas He that made me whole.

'Twas He that sought the lost,
That found the wandering sheep;
'Twas He that brought me to the fold,
'Tis He that still doth keep.

No more a wandering sheep
I love to be controlled
I love my tender Shepherd's voice
I love, I love the fold

No more a wayward child
I seek no more to roam
I love my heavenly Father's voice
I love, I love His home.

Horatius Bonar. (1808 - 1889)

Day 3

And the LORD said, Behold, there is a place by me,
and thou shalt stand upon a rock.
Exodus Ch33 v21

He brought me up also out of an horrible pit,
out of the miry clay, and set my feet upon a rock,
and established my goings.
Psalm 40 v2

And a man shall be as an hiding place from the wind,
and a covert from the tempest;
as rivers of water in a dry place,
as the shadow of a great rock in a weary land.
Isaiah Ch32 v2

The Lord Jesus said:
Therefore whosoever heareth these sayings of mine,
and doeth them, I will liken him unto a wise man,
which built his house upon a rock.
Matthew Ch7 v24

That Rock was Christ.
1st Corinthians Ch10 v4

Standing on the Rock of Ages,
The Rock that shall endure,
Unshaken by the tempest, eternal, firm and sure;

There is a safe retreat,
A refuge strong and free,
Amid the stormy billows of life's tempestuous sea.

Standing on the Rock of Ages,
We view the tranquil soul,
Untroubled by the tempest, or surging billows' roll;

Standing on the Rock of Ages,
No need have we to fear,
God banishes our sorrow, God wipes away our tear;

We're watching, we believe,
We trust His promise sure,
That crowns of joy are waiting for all His saints secure.

Fred Woodrow.

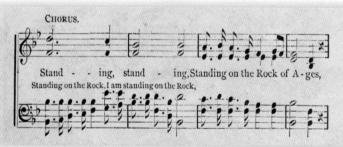

Day 4

*I*n 1762, so the story goes, Augustus Montague Toplady was travelling on horseback along Burrington Combe in the Mendip Hills of Somerset. At the time he was the minister of the nearby village of Blagdon. On this trip a sudden storm broke upon him with such fury that he was forced to seek immediate shelter from the driving rain and rising water. He found a cleft in a rock alongside the path he was travelling and managed to squeeze into position until the worst of the storm passed. Upon leaving the shelter of the cleft rock he was inspired to write what has become one of the world's greatest and most popular hymns *Rock of Ages*. Toplady who also wrote the popular hymn *A debtor to mercy alone* later ministered in London where he passed away in 1778 at the early age of 38.

At the cleft in which it is believed Augustus he took shelter is a simple plaque that reads "Rock of Ages: This rock derives its name from the well known hymn written about 1762 by the Rev. A.M. Toplady who was inspired whilst sheltering in this cleft during a storm."

How good it is to have a shelter to which to flee for safety when we realise that the storms of sickness, sin and sorrow are too fierce for us to face. The Lord Jesus, whose sufferings on the cross are so pointedly described in this hymn, offers an invitation to all who will trust Him as Saviour, "Come unto me, all ye that labour and are heavy laden, and I will give you rest." *Matthew Ch11 v28.*

Rock of Ages, cleft for me,
Let me hide myself in Thee;
Let the water and the blood,
From Thy wounded side which flowed,
Be of sin the double cure,
Save from wrath and make me pure.

Nothing in my hand I bring,
Simply to Thy cross I cling;
Naked, come to Thee for dress;
Helpless, look to Thee for grace;
Foul, I to the fountain fly;
wash me, Saviour, or I die.

While I draw this fleeting breath,
When my eyes shall close in death,
When I rise to worlds unknown,
And behold Thee on Thy throne,
Rock of Ages, cleft for me,
Let me hide myself in Thee.

Augustus Montague Toplady. (1740 - 1778)

Day 5

A God Full Of Compassion

But thou, O Lord, art a God full of compassion,
and gracious, longsuffering,
and plenteous in mercy and truth.
Psalm 86 v15

The LORD is gracious, and full of compassion;
slow to anger, and of great mercy.
Psalm 145 v8

But when he (Jesus) saw the multitudes,
he was moved with compassion on them,
because they fainted, and were scattered abroad,
as sheep having no shepherd.
Matthew Ch9 v36

And when the Lord saw her,
he had compassion on her,
and said unto her, Weep not.
Luke Ch7 v13

The Lord Jesus said:
But when he was yet a great way off,
his father saw him, and had compassion, and ran,
and fell on his neck, and kissed him.
Luke Ch15 v20

Great Is Thy Faithfulness

'Great is Thy faithfulness', O God my Father
There is no shadow of turning with Thee;
Thou changest not, Thy compassions, they fail not,
As Thou hast been, Thou forever will be.

'Great is Thy faithfulness', 'Great is Thy faithfulness'
Morning by morning new mercies I see;
All I have needed Thy hand hath provided
'Great is Thy faithfulness', Lord, unto me.

Pardon for sin and a peace that endureth,
Thine own dear presence to cheer and to guide;
Strength for today and bright hope for tomorrow,
Blessings all mine, with ten thousand beside.

Thomas Chisholm. (1866 - 1960)

13

Day 6

WHAT MANNER OF LOVE

Behold, what manner of love
the Father hath bestowed upon us,
that we should be called the sons of God.
1st John Ch3 v1

The Lord Jesus said:
For God so loved the world,
that he gave his only begotten Son,
that whosoever believeth in him should not perish,
but have everlasting life.
John Ch3 v16

The Son of God, who loved me,
and gave himself for me.
Galatians Ch2 v20

In this was manifested the love of God toward us,
because that God sent his only begotten Son into the world,
that we might live through him.
1st John Ch4 v9

The Love Of God

The love of God is greater far
Than tongue or pen can ever tell;
It goes beyond the highest star,
And reaches to the lowest hell;
The guilty pair, bowed down with care,
God gave His Son to win;
His erring child He reconciled,
And pardoned from his sin.

Oh, love of God, how rich and pure!
How measureless and strong!
It shall forevermore endure—
The saints' and angels' song.

Could we with ink the ocean fill,
And were the skies of parchment made,
Were every stalk on earth a quill,
And every man a scribe by trade;
To write the love of God above
Would drain the ocean dry;
Nor could the scroll contain the whole,
Though stretched from sky to sky.

Frederick Martin Lehman. (1868 – 1953)

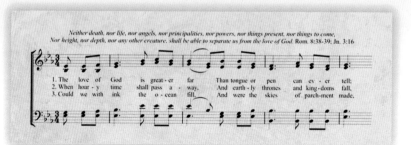

15

Day 7

Hold thou me up, and I shall be safe.
Psalm 119 v117

The fear of man bringeth a snare:
but whoso putteth his trust in the LORD shall be safe.
Proverbs Ch29 v25

I would seek unto God,
and unto God would I commit my cause:
Which doeth great things and unsearchable;
marvellous things without number:
Who giveth rain upon the earth,
and sendeth waters upon the fields:
To set up on high those that be low;
that those which mourn may be exalted to safety.
Job Ch5 v8-11

I will both lay me down in peace, and sleep:
for thou, LORD, only makest me dwell in safety.
Psalm 4 v8

Safety is of the Lord.
Proverbs Ch21 v31

"THE NAME OF THE LORD IS A STRONG TOWER

Safe in Jehovah's keeping, Led by His glorious arm,
God is Himself my refuge, A present help from harm.
Fears may at times distress me,
Griefs may my soul annoy;
God is my strength and portion,
God my exceeding joy.

Safe in Jehovah's keeping, Safe in temptation's hour,
Safe in the midst of perils, Kept by almighty power.
Safe when the tempest rages,
Safe though the night be long;
E'en when my sky is darkest
God is my strength and song.

Sure is Jehovah's promise, Naught can my hope assail;
Here is my soul's sure anchor, Entered within the veil.
Blest in His love eternal,
What can I want beside!
Safe through the blood that cleanseth,
Safe in the Christ that died.

Sir Robert Anderson. (1841–1918)

HE RIGHTEOUS RUNNETH INTO IT, AND IS SAFE."
PROVERBS 18:10

CAREST THOU NOT?

"And there arose a great storm of wind,
and the waves beat into the ship, so that it was now full.
And he was in the hinder part of the ship, asleep on a pillow:
and they awake him, and say unto him, Master,
carest thou not that we perish?"
Mark Ch4 v37-38

*F*or a moment of time the disciples lost sight of all hope when fear of perishing came upon them. They had forgotten His **promise**: *"Let us pass over to the other side,"* and they had forgotten who was **present** with them: *"He was in the ship."* They also did not realise His **power**, which He was about to demonstrate. All they could think of at that moment was ... *"We Perish!"* But this was not to be the case as we shall see.

They did get one vital thing right however; and that was that they came to Jesus with their dilemma. After all, there wasn't anyone else to turn to, and nobody else was needed anyway! For a moment they doubted His care but He never rebuked them for this, instead He arose and rebuked the storm with the power of His words. The Bible tells us: *"And the wind ceased, and there was a great calm."* Mark Ch4 v39.

God not only cares for, but loves His people beyond human comprehension, and demonstrated this: *"God commendeth his love toward us, in that, while we were yet sinners, Christ died for us."* Romans Ch5 v8. If ever we are to come into the benefit of His care we must agree with Him about our sin and repent of it, fully trusting in His beloved Son for time and for eternity. You can count on the faithful **promise** of His **presence**, and His **power** to keep and preserve His people until one day soon when we see Him face to face.

He Careth for Me

The storm, in attempting to spoil my peace,
And toss my small bark on the sea,
As the troubles of life came upon me like waves;
I learnt that He careth for me.

I then couldn't see it; for dark was the night
That hid my dear Lord from my view.
The howl of the wind, it unsteadied my path,
And my cares and my fears they all grew.

He seemed to be sleeping, I felt so alone!
Then I thought: "though He sleeps, He's still there."
I trusted His promise to see me right through,
And I cast upon Him all my care.

He rose up to strengthen my tottering faith,
And commanded my storm to be still.
I learnt in the storm that He cares for my soul,
And His purpose in me He'll fulfil.

AleB

Day 8

*C*hristian vocalist Ira Sankey tells the story of a girl named Maggie who had trusted the Lord Jesus as her Saviour during Gospel meetings conducted by Dwight Moody and himself eight years previously. Since then she had become seriously ill and sadly passed away. Just before dying she asked her mother for her hymn book, stating 'I want to sing.'

'You are too weak to sing,' her mother replied.

'But I want to sing one more song,' she replied, 'will you please turn to the twenty-fifth hymn, *Safe in the Arms of Jesus*?' So her mother found the song and her daughter began to sing these lines:

'Hark, 'tis the voice of angels borne in a song to me, Over the fields of glory, over the jasper sea.'

Her voice then seemed to fail, and she said, 'Mother, please lift me up.' Lifted up in her mother's loving arms she raised her eyes to heaven and whispered: 'Jesus, I am coming.'

The doctor, who was standing by her side, asked: 'How can you sing when you are so weak?'

She replied: 'Jesus helps me to sing.' And with these words upon her lips she went to Heaven.

A few days later at her funeral the precious little hymn book that had brought Maggie such comfort was laid upon the girl's breast and buried with her.

Safe in the arms of Jesus,
Safe on His gentle breast,
There by His love o'ershaded,
Sweetly my soul doth rest.
Hark! 'tis the voice of angels,
Borne in a song to me,
Over the fields of glory,
Over the crystal sea.

Safe in the arms of Jesus,
Safe from corroding care,
Safe from the world's temptations,
Sin cannot harm me there.
Free from the blight of sorrow,
Free from my doubts and fears;
Only a few more trials,
Only a few more tears.

Jesus, my heart's dear Refuge,
Jesus has died for me;
Firm on the Rock of Ages
Ever my trust shall be.
Here let me wait with patience,
Wait till the night is o'er,
Wait till I see the morning
Break on the golden shore.

Frances Jane (Fanny) Crosby. (1820 - 1915)

Day 9

I am weary with my groaning;
all the night make I my bed to swim;
I water my couch with my tears.
Psalm 6 v6

Thus saith the LORD … I have heard thy prayer,
I have seen thy tears:
2nd Kings Ch20 v5

For thou hast delivered my soul from death,
mine eyes from tears, and my feet from falling.
Psalm 116 v8

(The Lord Jesus) Who in the days of his flesh,
when he had offered up prayers and supplications
with strong crying and tears unto him that was able
to save him from death … and was heard.
Hebrews Ch5 v7

And God shall wipe away all tears from their eyes;
and there shall be no more death, neither sorrow, nor
crying, neither shall there be any more pain.
Revelation Ch21 v4

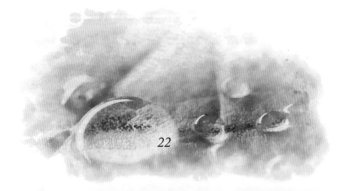

When gathering clouds around I view,
And days are dark, and friends are few,
On Him I lean, who, not in vain,
Experienced every human pain;
He sees my wants, allays my fears,
And counts and treasures up my tears.

If vexing thoughts within me rise
And, sore dismayed, my spirit dies,
Still He, who once vouchsafed to bear
The sickening anguish of despair,
Shall sweetly soothe, shall gently dry,
The throbbing heart, the streaming eye.

When sorrowing o'er some stone I bend,
Which covers what was once a friend,
And from his voice, his hand, his smile,
Divides me for a little while,
Thou, Saviour, mark'st the tears I shed,
For Thou didst weep once o'er the dead.

And O, when I have safely passed,
Through every conflict but the last;
Still, still unchanging, watch beside
My painful bed, for Thou hast died;
Then point to realms of cloudless day,
And wipe the latest tear way.

Sir Robert Grant. (1780 - 1838)

Day 10

THERE IS A FRIEND

Faithful are the wounds of a friend.
Proverbs Ch27 v6

A friend loveth at all times.
Proverbs Ch17 v17

The Lord Jesus said:
The Son of man is come eating and drinking; and ye say,
Behold a gluttonous man, and a winebibber,
a friend of publicans and sinners!
Luke Ch7 v34

The Lord Jesus said:
Greater love hath no man than this,
that a man lay down his life for his friends.
John Ch15 v13

There is a friend that sticketh closer than a brother.
Proverbs Ch18 v24

He is altogether lovely.
This is my beloved, and this is my friend.
Song of Solomon Ch5 v16

"I WILL NEVER LEAVE THE

24

Oh, what blessed sweet com-mun - ion, Je - sus is a friend of mine.

A Friend Of Jesus

A friend of Jesus! Oh, what bliss
That one so weak as I
Should ever have a Friend like this
To lead me to the sky!

A Friend when other friendships cease,
A Friend when others fail,
A Friend who gives me joy and peace,
A Friend when foes assail!

A Friend when sickness lays me low,
A Friend when death draws near,
A Friend as through the vale I go,
A Friend to help and cheer!

A Friend when life's short race is o'er
A Friend when earth is past,
A Friend to meet on Heaven's shore,
A Friend when home at last!

Joseph C Ludgate. (1864 - 1947)

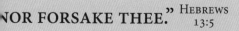

NOR FORSAKE THEE." HEBREWS
13:5

Day 11

*T*wo men stood watching a man carrying an axe. One commented, 'That man is happy. I wish I could know his joy. Perhaps I can get him to cut my winter's supply of wood?' The second replied, 'That's Joseph Scriven. He cuts wood for those who are unable to cut their own.' Joseph was born in 1819 in Banbridge, Northern Ireland. Early in his life he trusted the Lord Jesus Christ as his Saviour. After qualifying as a teacher he worked in his home town becoming engaged to be married. The day before his wedding, his fiancé fell from her horse whilst crossing the river Bann and was tragically drowned. Overcome with grief, he left Ireland to start a new life in Canada, settling in Port Hope, Ontario. Here Scriven heard that his mother was very ill and to encourage her, wrote her a little poem called *Pray without ceasing*, which would become known as *What a Friend We Have in Jesus*. In 1860 Scriven was engaged to Eliza Roche. However weeks before the wedding, Eliza contracted pneumonia and died. A shattered Scriven turned to the only thing that had anchored him during his life - his faith. He put all his efforts into preaching the gospel and helping the needy around Port Hope.

After Scriven's death, evangelist Dwight L. Moody came across his powerful poem and began using it in his meetings as a hymn thereby giving it worldwide recognition.

What a friend we have in Jesus,
All our sins and griefs to bear!
What a privilege to carry
Everything to God in prayer!
Oh, what peace we often forfeit,
Oh, what needless pain we bear,
All because we do not carry
Everything to God in prayer!

Have we trials and temptations?
Is there trouble anywhere?
We should never be discouraged -
Take it to the Lord in prayer.
Can we find a friend so faithful,
Who will all our sorrows share?
Jesus knows our every weakness;
Take it to the Lord in prayer.

Are we weak and heavy-laden,
Cumbered with a load of care?
Precious Saviour, still our refuge -
Take it to the Lord in prayer.
Do thy friends despise, forsake thee?
Take it to the Lord in prayer!
In His arms He'll take and shield thee,
Thou wilt find a solace there.

Joseph M. Scriven. (1819 - 1886)

Day 12

Blessed be the God and Father
of our Lord Jesus Christ,
which according to his abundant mercy
hath begotten us again unto a lively hope
by the resurrection of Jesus Christ from the dead.

1st Peter Ch1 v3

Looking for that blessed hope,
and the glorious appearing
of the great God and our Saviour Jesus Christ.

Titus Ch2 v13

Now the God of hope fill you with all joy and peace
in believing, that ye may abound in hope,
through the power of the Holy Ghost.

Romans Ch15 v13

I wait for the LORD, my soul doth wait,
and in his word do I hope.

Psalm 130 v5

Which hope we have as an anchor of the soul,
both sure and stedfast,
and which entereth into that within the veil.

Hebrews Ch6 v19

My hope is built on nothing less
Than Jesus' blood and righteousness;
I dare not trust the sweetest frame,
But wholly lean on Jesus' name.
On Christ, the solid Rock, I stand;
All other ground is sinking sand.

When darkness veils His lovely face,
I rest on His unchanging grace;
In every high and stormy gale
My anchor holds within the veil.
On Christ, the solid Rock, I stand;
All other ground is sinking sand.

His oath, His covenant, His blood,
Support me in the whelming flood.
When all around my soul gives way,
He then is all my hope and stay.
On Christ, the solid Rock, I stand;
All other ground is sinking sand.

Edward Mote (1797 - 1874)

Day 13

The LORD is my rock, and my fortress,
and my deliverer; The God of my rock;
in him will I trust:
he is my shield, and the horn of my salvation,
my high tower, and my refuge, my saviour;
thou savest me from violence.

2nd Samuel Ch22 v2-3

God is our refuge and strength,
a very present help in trouble.

Psalm 46 v1

Be merciful unto me, O God, be merciful unto me:
for my soul trusteth in thee:
yea, in the shadow of thy wings will I make my refuge,
until these calamities be overpast.

Psalm 57 v1

Trust in him at all times; ye people,
pour out your heart before him:
God is a refuge for us.

Psalm 62 v8

Say, where is thy refuge, my brother,
And what is thy prospect today?
Why toil for the wealth that will perish,
The treasures that rust and decay?

Oh, think of thy soul, that forever
Must live on eternity's shore,
When thou in the dust art forgotten,
When pleasure can charm thee no more.

The Master is calling thee, brother,
In tones of compassion and love,
To feel that sweet rapture of pardon,
And lay up thy treasure above;

Oh, kneel at the cross where He suffered,
To ransom thy soul from the grave,
The arm of His mercy will hold Thee,
The arm that is mighty to save.

Then slight not the warning repeated
With all the bright moments that roll,
Nor say, when the harvest is ended,
That no one hath cared for thy soul.

Frances Jane (Fanny) Crosby. (1820 - 1915)

Day 14

But God, who is rich in mercy,
for his great love wherewith he loved us,
Even when we were dead in sins,
hath quickened us together with Christ,
(by grace ye are saved)
And hath raised us up together, and made us sit together
in heavenly places in Christ Jesus ...
For by grace are ye saved through faith;
and that not of yourselves: it is the gift of God:
Not of works, lest any man should boast.

Ephesians Ch2 v4-5, 8-9

Seeing then that we have a great high priest,
that is passed into the heavens, Jesus the Son of God,
let us hold fast our profession.
For we have not an high priest which cannot be touched
with the feeling of our infirmities;
but was in all points tempted like as we are,
yet without sin.
Let us therefore come boldly unto the throne of grace,
that we may obtain mercy,
and find grace to help in time of need.

Hebrews Ch4 v14-16

The door of God's mercy is open,
To all who are weary of sin.
And Jesus is patiently waiting,
Still waiting, to welcome you in.

So many who hear the glad message
Will never its mandates obey,
But turn from the precious, dear pleadings,
And wilfully wander away.

Sad hearts there will surely be mourning
Outside of the gateway of life,
And praying to Him they rejected
When earth with gay pleasures was rife.

The door of God's mercy is open,
Invitingly open to all
Who list to the voice of the Master,
And hearing shall heed His sweet call.

Ellen Oliver Van Fleet. (1842 - 1893)

JUST .... STANDING!

"For a small moment have I forsaken thee; but with great mercies will I gather thee." Isaiah Ch54 v7

The field that was once clothed with beautiful golden wheat was now dotted with decorative stooks left to stand.

If the wheat had a voice perhaps it would say something like this: "Why have I been cut down and left to stand against the elements and forgotten?"

Does this sound familiar? Do you feel as if you also have been left - just ... standing?

The wheat has to go through a process of waiting under the heat of the sun if ever the wheat kernels are going to be usable. Without this process it would be no good for human consumption, or for re-sowing for future crops. Perhaps you are in the process of learning the unspeakable wealth of waiting on the Lord.

The heat of oppression or the winds of adversity are getting you down - but wait! Every ounce of your being is telling you that something has gone wrong - but wait! Don't fret, don't struggle, don't allow yourself to be overwhelmed by your circumstances - just wait!

The Lord knows your situation and your inmost feelings, and you may have been set aside by divine appointment. Sometimes it is necessary for God to place His children in the dark, or make them stand and wait for a while in order to prepare them for receiving treasures of immeasurable value. And those treasures might just be appreciations of Himself you would never have learned otherwise - and yours to keep for eternity!

So, be comforted to know that like all uncomfortable situations, this also will come to pass!

Wait on Him
(Isaiah 40:31)

Picture the eagle flying high,
None can pluck him from the sky.
And with the strength that fills his wings
He's not tied down by earthly things.

The promise is to us so sweet,
To trust the Lord, our strength to meet,
Our heart's affections God-ward rise,
And see as He does from the skies:

That earthly worries have no hold
On one who waits upon his God.
For like the eagle in the air
Our souls take flight above the care -

That once did bind our soul to earth,
And gave to us but little worth.
Great strength to those who on Him call,
And wait on Him, their all in all.

AleB

Day 15

And the child (Jesus) grew, and waxed strong in spirit,
filled with wisdom:
and the grace of God was upon him.

Luke Ch2 v40

And the Word (The Lord Jesus) was made flesh,
and dwelt among us, (and we beheld his glory,
the glory as of the only begotten of the Father,)
full of grace and truth.

John Ch1 v14

For ye know the grace of our Lord Jesus Christ,
that, though he was rich,
yet for your sakes he became poor,
that ye through his poverty might be rich.

2nd Corinthians Ch8 v9

Being justified freely by his grace
through the redemption that is in Christ Jesus.

Romans Ch3 v24

My grace is sufficient for thee:
for my strength is made perfect in weakness.

2nd Corinthians Ch12 v9

By Grace Are Ye Saved

In grace the holy God
Did full salvation plan,
Deciding in His sovereign grace
To save rebellious man.

This grace of God appears
In Jesus Christ His Son;
He, lifted on the cross of shame,
The grace of God makes known.

To all who do believe
In God, thro' Christ revealed
By grace, they full salvation have,
And 'sons of God' are sealed.

Daniel W. Whittle. (1840–1901)

Day 16

AMAZING GRACE

*W*hen Army Chaplain Henry Gerecke stepped into the cell of Joachim Ribbentrop in the early hours of 16th October 1946 he was aware that God had been at work with the man sitting before him. Ribbentrop, one-time Foreign Minister in Hitler's Nazi government, knew that Gerecke and the guards were coming to lead him to the gallows where he would pay the ultimate price for his part in the crimes committed by that regime. However during his yearlong trail at Nuremburg Ribbentrop had undergone a remarkable change. Having been given a Bible, initially so that he could point out all its errors and inconsistencies, Ribbentrop had discovered that remarkable book offered, even to someone like him, the opportunity of forgiveness of sin and an eternal home in Heaven. He realised too that such promises were centred in the person and work of the Lord Jesus Christ. Having trusted him as Saviour he was now a recipient of the Grace (unmerited favour) of God. As he prepared to walk to the scaffold he asked Henry Gerecke to pray with him stating, 'I wish you to know that I am placing all my faith in the Lamb of God who takes away the sin of the world!' A few minutes later standing with the rope around his neck he addressed Pastor Gerecke, 'I'll see you again.'

Such a change in life and destiny is what John Newton had written about in his hymn *Amazing Grace*. He too had been delivered from a life of great sin by the death, burial and resurrection of Jesus Christ.

Amazing Grace!

Amazing grace! How sweet the sound
That saved a wretch like me!
I once was lost, but now am found;
Was blind, but now I see.

'Twas grace that taught my heart to fear,
And grace my fears relieved;
How precious did that grace appear
The hour I first believed!

Through many dangers, toils and snares,
I have already come;
'Tis grace hath brought me safe thus far,
And grace will lead me home.

When we've been there ten thousand years,
Bright shining as the sun,
We've no less days to sing God's praise
Than when we'd first begun.

John Newton. (1725 - 1807)

AMAZING
G*od's* R*iches* A*t* C*hrist's* E*xpense*

Day 17

FATHER, FORGIVE

And when they were come to the place,
which is called Calvary,
there they crucified him, and the malefactors,
one on the right hand, and the other on the left.
Then said Jesus, Father, forgive them;
for they know not what they do.

Luke Ch23 v33-34

But God commendeth his love toward us,
in that, while we were yet sinners, Christ died for us.

Romans Ch5 v8

For I delivered unto you first of all
that which I also received,
how that Christ died for our sins
according to the scriptures;
And that he was buried,
and that he rose again the third day
according to the scriptures.

1st Corinthians Ch15 v3-4

"IF WE CONFESS OUR SINS, HE IS FAITHFUI

Not what my hands have done
Can save my guilty soul;
Not what my toiling flesh has borne
Can make my spirit whole.
Not what I feel or do can give me peace with God;
Not all my prayers and sighs and tears
Can bear my awful load.

Thy work alone, O Christ,
Can ease this weight of sin;
Thy blood alone, O Lamb of God,
Can give me peace within.
Thy love to me, O God, not mine, O Lord, to Thee,
Can rid me of this dark unrest,
And set my spirit free.

I bless the Christ of God;
I rest on love divine;
And with unfaltering lip and heart
I call this Saviour mine.
His cross dispels each doubt; I bury in His tomb
Each thought of unbelief and fear,
Each lingering shade of gloom.

Horatius Bonar. (1808 - 1889)

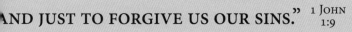

AND JUST TO FORGIVE US OUR SINS." 1 JOHN 1:9

Day 18

The LORD will give strength unto his people;
the LORD will bless his people with peace.
Psalm 29 v11

For unto us a child is born, unto us a son is given:
and the government shall be upon his shoulder:
and his name shall be called Wonderful, Counsellor,
The mighty God, The everlasting Father,
The Prince of Peace.
Isaiah Ch9 v6

But he was wounded for our transgressions,
he was bruised for our iniquities:
the chastisement of our peace was upon him;
and with his stripes we are healed.
All we like sheep have gone astray;
we have turned every one to his own way;
and the LORD hath laid on him the iniquity of us all.
Isaiah Ch53 v5-6

The Lord Jesus said:
Thy faith hath saved thee; go in peace.
Luke Ch7 v50

The Lord Jesus said:
Peace I leave with you, my peace I give unto you:
not as the world giveth, give I unto you.
Let not your heart be troubled, neither let it be afraid.
John Ch14 v27

Peace, Perfect Peace

Peace, perfect peace, in this dark world of sin?
The blood of Jesus whispers peace within.
Peace, perfect peace, by thronging duties pressed?
To do the will of Jesus, this is rest.

Peace, perfect peace, with sorrows surging round?
On Jesus' bosom naught but calm is found.
Peace, perfect peace, with loved ones far away?
In Jesus' keeping we are safe, and they.

Peace, perfect peace, our future all unknown?
Jesus we know, and He is on the throne.
Peace, perfect peace, death shadowing us and ours?
Jesus has vanquished death and all its powers.

It is enough: earth's struggles soon shall cease,
And Jesus call us to Heaven's perfect peace.

Edward H. Bickersteth. (1825–1906)

Day 19

All Scripture is given by inspiration of God,
and is profitable for doctrine,
for reproof, for correction,
for instruction in righteousness.
2nd Timothy Ch3 v16

For whatsoever things were written aforetime
were written for our learning,
that we through patience
and comfort of the scriptures might have hope.
Romans Ch15 v4

For ever, O LORD, thy word is settled in heaven.
Psalm 119 v89

Thy word is true from the beginning:
and every one of thy righteous judgments
endureth for ever.
Psalm 119 v160

Thy word is a lamp unto my feet,
and a light unto my path.
Psalm 119 v105

The Lord Jesus said:
Search the scriptures;
for in them ye think ye have eternal life:
and they are they which testify of me.
John Ch5 v39

Oh, wonderful, wonderful Word of the Lord!
True wisdom its pages unfold;
And though we may read them a thousand times o'er,
They never, no never, grow old!

Each line hath a treasure, each promise a pearl,
That all if they will may secure;
And we know that when time and the world pass away,
God's Word shall forever endure.

Oh, wonderful, wonderful Word of the Lord!
The lamp that our Father above
So kindly has lighted to teach us the way
That leads to the arms of His love!

Its warnings, its counsels, are faithful and just;
Its judgments are perfect and pure;
And we know that when time and the world pass away,
God's Word shall forever endure.

Oh, wonderful, wonderful Word of the Lord!
Our only salvation is there;
It carries conviction down deep in the heart,
And shows us ourselves as we are.

It tells of a Saviour, and points to the cross,
Where pardon we now may secure;
For we know that when time and the world pass away,
God's Word shall forever endure.

Frances Jane (Fanny) Crosby. (1820 – 1915)

Day 20

PLEASURES FOR EVERMORE

The Lord Jesus said:
Let not your heart be troubled:
ye believe in God, believe also in me.
In my Father's house are many mansions:
if it were not so, I would have told you.
I go to prepare a place for you.
And if I go and prepare a place for you,
I will come again,
and receive you unto myself;
that where I am, there ye may be also.
John Ch14 v1-3

Thou wilt shew me the path of life:
in thy presence is fulness of joy;
at thy right hand there are pleasures for evermore.
Psalm 16 v11

And God shall wipe away all tears from their eyes;
and there shall be no more death,
neither sorrow, nor crying,
neither shall there be any more pain:
for the former things are passed away.
And he that sat upon the throne said,
Behold, I make all things new. And he said unto me,
Write: for these words are true and faithful.
Revelation Ch21 v4-5

Shall I Meet You Up There?

There's a beautiful home far up in the sky,
And mansions prepared by our Saviour on high;
He wants me to live in that country so fair,
And when I'm in glory, Shall I meet you up there?

In that beautiful land no sorrow will come,
We shall sing hallelujah around the bright throne;
A beautiful robe and a crown we shall wear,
And live there with Jesus. Shall I meet you up there?

No night shall be there, it is one endless day,
No tears will be shed, God will wipe them away;
No sickness and dying, no pain we shall bear,
No parting with loved ones. Shall I meet you up there?

John B Vaughan. (1862 - 1918)

Day 21

The days of our years are threescore years and ten;
and if by reason of strength they be fourscore years,
yet is their strength labour and sorrow; for it is soon cut off,
and we fly away.
Psalm 90 v10

Is it nothing to you, all ye that pass by?
behold, and see if there be any sorrow
like unto my sorrow,
which is done unto me, wherewith the LORD hath afflicted
me in the day of his fierce anger.
Lamentations Ch1 v12

He is despised and rejected of men; a man of sorrows, and
acquainted with grief:
and we hid as it were our faces from him;
he was despised, and we esteemed him not.
Surely he hath borne our griefs,
and carried our sorrow:
yet we did esteem him stricken,
smitten of God, and afflicted.
Isaiah Ch53 v 3-4

Therefore the redeemed of the LORD shall return,
and come with singing unto Zion;
and everlasting joy shall be upon their head:
they shall obtain gladness and joy;
and sorrow and mourning shall flee away.
Isaiah Ch51 v11

O Let Him Whose Sorrow

O let him whose sorrow no relief can find,
Trust in God, and borrow ease for heart and mind.
Where the mourner weeping sheds the secret tear,
God His watch is keeping, though none else is near.

God will never leave thee, all thy wants He knows,
Feels the pains that grieve thee, sees thy cares and woes;
Raise thine eyes to Heaven when thy spirits quail,
When, by tempests driven, heart and courage fail.

All thy woe and sadness, in this world below,
Balance not the gladness thou in Heaven shalt know,
When thy gracious Saviour in the realms above
Crowns thee with His favour, fills thee with His love.

John B. Dykes. (1823 - 1876)

SOMETHING FOR GOD

*W*hy do we have to go through times of trials, and are they absolutely necessary? Well, the answer to that question is an absolute 'yes', if ever we are going to grow in our faith and in our appreciation of the Lord Jesus who, *"loved me, and gave himself for me."* (Galatians Ch2 v20). He didn't go to the cross to save us from our sin only to leave us with a saved soul and nothing else! The Bible tells us that: *"He which hath begun a good work in you will perform it until the day of Jesus Christ."* (Philippians Ch1 v6).

The work He begins when someone believes on and trusts in Him, He continues daily in the life of those who seek to follow and obey Him. He desires to produce Christ-like character in us, so that when we finally arrive home in heaven, either through death or when our Lord and Saviour comes for His beloved people as He promised - we will not go to Him empty handed.

But what could we possibly give to God that He will value? Only that which endures the flame as it were! Gold, silver, and precious stones endure the crucible and shine greater the more intense the heat, but wood, hay, and stubble will leave nothing but ashes.

We all have the potential to give something He will treasure, and now is the time in which to make that eternal investment. The trials we have to go through draw us closer to Him and burn away all that doesn't shine.

So, be encouraged fellow sufferers to know that although *"weeping may endure for a night ... joy cometh in the morning."* (Psalm 30 v5). And the morning is almost upon us.

A Speck of Gold

Oh Lord! Within my darkest hour,
When stormy clouds hang low,
When disappointments are my lot;
It cheers my heart to know -

Thou Rock, higher than I, and so
The storm can't reach this realm.
This peaceful place where I may go
When I am overwhelmed.

Yes, Thou art there, always so near.
And with Thine outstretched arm:
Thou liftest up this soul of mine,
And givest me great calm.

Thy presence is a balm to me
As I go through each trial.
One day I'll understand - after
I've suffered for a while.

Thou hast designed each trial of fire
My dross to burn away.
O, may it leave a speck of gold
To give to Thee one day!

AleB

"WHEN HE HATH TRIED ME, I SHALL COME FORTH AS GOLD" JOB 23:10

Day 22

Be not far from me; for trouble is near;
for there is none to help.
But be not thou far from me, O LORD: O my strength,
haste thee to help me.
Psalm 22 v11-19

Our soul waiteth for the LORD:
he is our help and our shield.
Psalm 33 v20

Fear thou not; for I am with thee: be not dismayed;
for I am thy God: I will strengthen thee;
yea, I will help thee; yea, I will uphold thee
with the right hand of my righteousness.
For I the LORD thy God will hold thy right hand,
saying unto thee, Fear not; I will help thee.
Isaiah Ch41 v10-13

Let us therefore come boldly unto the throne of grace,
that we may obtain mercy,
and find grace to help in time of need.
Hebrews Ch4 v16

O help us, Lord, each hour of need
Thy heavenly succour give;
Help us in thought, and word, and deed,
Each hour on earth we live.

O help us, when our spirits bleed
With contrite anguish sore,
And when our hearts are cold and dead,
O help us, Lord, the more.

O help us, through the prayer of faith
More firmly to believe;
For still the more the servant hath,
The more shall he receive.

O help us, Jesus! from on high,
We know no help but Thee;
Oh! help us so to live and die
As Thine in Heav'n to be.

Henry H. Milman. (1791 - 1868)

Day 23

Fear ye not, stand still, and see the salvation of the LORD,
which he will shew to you to day.
Exodus Ch14 v13

Be it known unto you all, and to all the people of Israel,
that by the name of Jesus Christ of Nazareth,
whom ye crucified, whom God raised from the dead,
even by him doth this man stand here before you whole.
Neither is there salvation in any other:
for there is none other name under heaven
given among men,
whereby we must be saved.
Acts Ch4 v10-12

For I am not ashamed of the gospel of Christ:
for it is the power of God unto salvation
to every one that believeth.
Romans Ch1 v16

For God hath not appointed us to wrath,
but to obtain salvation by our Lord Jesus Christ.
1st Thessalonians Ch5 v9

How shall we escape, if we neglect so great salvation?
Hebrews Ch2 v3

O boundless salvation! deep ocean of love,
O fullness of mercy, Christ brought from above,
The whole world redeeming, so rich and so free,
Now flowing for all men, now come, roll over me!

My sins they are many, their stains are so deep,
And bitter the tears of remorse that I weep;
But useless is weeping; thou great crimson sea,
Thy waters can cleanse me, come, roll over me!

The tide is now flowing, I'm touching the wave,
I hear the loud call of the Mighty to Save;
My faith's growing bolder, delivered I'll be;
I plunge 'neath the waters, they roll over me.

And now, hallelujah! the rest of my days
Shall gladly be spent in promoting His praise
Who opened His bosom to pour out this sea
Of boundless salvation for you and for me.

William Booth. (1829 - 1912)

Day 24

*O*n 22nd November 1873 the paddle steamer 'Ville du Havre' carrying 313 passengers and crew collided with the Scottish clipper 'Loch Earn' sinking in twelve minutes. Tragically only 61 passengers and 26 members of the crew were able to be rescued from the freezing waters of the Atlantic Ocean. On board the 'Ville du Havre' that night was Anna Spafford, wife of Chicago lawyer Horatio Spafford, along with their four daughters Annie, Maggie, Bessie and Tanetta. After the sinking, an unconscious Anna was pulled from the water by the crew of the 'Loch Earn'. There was however no sign of her four daughters. Upon regaining consciousness Mrs Spafford said, 'God gave me four daughters. Now they have been taken from me. Someday I will understand why.' On arrival in Cardiff (Wales) Anna sent a telegram to her husband reading, 'Saved alone. What shall I do?' Her husband immediately set sail across the Atlantic to be at his wife's side. As he passed over the place of the tragedy, he composed the well-loved hymn *It is well with my soul*. Mrs Spafford's question to her husband 'What shall I do' is strikingly like one asked many years before in the Bible, "What must I do to be saved?" The answer today is just the same, "Believe on the Lord Jesus Christ, and thou shalt be saved!" *Acts Ch16 v31*. In other words rest on all that Christ has done upon the cross and through His resurrection for your soul's salvation. Then you too can sing in Heaven through all eternity 'It is well with my soul!'

When peace, like a river, attendeth my way,
When sorrows like sea billows roll;
Whatever my lot, Thou has taught me to say,
It is well, it is well, with my soul.

Though Satan should buffet,
Though trials should come,
Let this blest assurance control,
That Christ hath regarded my helpless estate,
And hath shed His own blood for my soul.

My sin - oh, the bliss of this glorious thought -
My sin - not in part but the whole,
Is nailed to the cross, and I bear it no more,
Praise the Lord, praise the Lord, O my soul!

But, Lord, 'tis for Thee, for Thy coming we wait,
The sky, not the grave, is our goal;
Oh trump of the angel! Oh voice of the Lord!
Blessèd hope, blessèd rest of my soul!

Horatio Gates Spafford. (1828 - 1888)

Day 25

And on the seventh day God ended his work
which he had made; and he rested on the seventh day
from all his work which he had made.
Genesis Ch2 v2

Rest in the LORD, and wait patiently for him:
fret not thyself because of him who prospereth in his way,
because of the man who bringeth wicked devices to pass.
Psalm 37 v7

The Lord Jesus said:
Come unto me, all ye that labour and are heavy laden,
and I will give you rest.
Take my yoke upon you, and learn of me;
for I am meek and lowly in heart:
and ye shall find rest unto your souls.
Matthew Ch11 v28-29

There remaineth therefore a rest to the people of God.
Hebrews Ch4 v9

And I heard a voice from heaven saying unto me, Write,
Blessed are the dead which die in the Lord from henceforth:
Yea, saith the Spirit,
that they may rest from their labours;
and their works do follow them.
Revelation Ch14 v13

Brother, art thou worn and weary,
Tempted, tried, and sore oppressed?
Listen to the word of Jesus,
Come unto Me, and rest!

Oh, He knows the dark forebodings
Of the conscience troubled breast,
And to such His word is given,
Come unto Me, and rest!

To the Lord bring all your burden,
Put the promise to the test;
Hear Him say, your Burden Bearer,
Come unto Me, and rest!

If in sorrow thou art weeping,
Grieving for the loved ones missed,
Surely then to you He whispers,
Come unto Me, and rest!

Trust to Him for all thy future,
He will give thee what is best;
Why then fear when He is saying,
Come unto Me, and rest!

Daniel W. Whittle. (1840 - 1901)

Day 26

The harvest is past, the summer is ended,
and we are not saved.
Jeremiah Ch8 v20

Who then can be saved?
Mark Ch10 v26

Look unto me, and be ye saved, all the ends of the earth:
for I am God, and there is none else.
Isaiah Ch45 v22

God our Saviour; Who will have all men to be saved,
and to come unto the knowledge of the truth.
For there is one God, and one mediator
between God and men, the man Christ Jesus;
Who gave himself a ransom for all,
to be testified in due time.
1st Timothy Ch2 v3-6

Believe on the Lord Jesus Christ, and thou shalt be saved.
Acts Ch16 v31

That if thou shalt confess with thy mouth the Lord Jesus,
and shalt believe in thine heart
that God hath raised him from the dead,
thou shalt be saved.
Romans Ch10 v9

"IF I HAD A **THOUSAND** SOULS I WOULD
GLADLY GIVE THEM **ALL** TO CHRIST."
-Author Unknown

Saved to the uttermost: I am the Lord's;
Jesus my Saviour salvation affords;
Gives me His Spirit, a witness within,
Whispering of pardon, and saving from sin.

Saved to the uttermost: Jesus is near;
Keeping me safely, He casteth out fear;
Trusting His promises, now I am blest;
Leaning upon Him, how sweet is my rest.

Saved to the uttermost: this I can say,
Once all was darkness, but now it is day;
Beautiful visions of glory I see,
Jesus in brightness revealed unto me.

Saved to the uttermost; cheerfully sing
Loud halleluiahs to Jesus my king;
Ransomed and pardoned, redeemed by His blood,
Cleansed from unrighteousness; glory to God!

William James Kirkpatrick. (1838 - 1921)

Day 27

The Lord Jesus said:
Because thou sayest, I am rich, and increased with goods,
and have need of nothing;
and knowest not that thou art wretched, and miserable,
and poor, and blind, and naked:
Revelation Ch3 v17

Bow down thine ear, O LORD, hear me:
for I am poor and needy.
Psalm 86 v1

The Lord Jesus said:
Therefore take no thought, saying, What shall we eat? or,
What shall we drink? or, Wherewithal shall we be clothed?
(For after all these things do the Gentiles seek:)
for your heavenly Father knoweth
that ye have need of all these things.
But seek ye first the kingdom of God,
and his righteousness;
and all these things shall be added unto you.
Matthew Ch6 v31-33

But my God shall supply all your need
according to his riches in glory by Christ Jesus.
Philippians Ch4 v19

I was poor as the poorest outcast from the fold,
I sank by the wayside with hunger and cold;
But He bade me look up, all His riches behold;
O the wealth of the world is Jesus.

I was poor as the poorest, I wandered alone,
No dwelling I had, and my pillow a stone;
But I heard someone whisper, My child, still My own;
Now the peace of my heart is Jesus.

I was poor as the poorest; He came from the sky
With love that was deathless for sinners to die;
And He bled on the cross, and my heart said, 'Tis I;
Now the love in my soul is Jesus.

I was poor as the poorest till Jesus stooped low
And washed all my sins of the whiteness of snow;
And so that is the reason I love Him, you know;
O the wealth of the world is Jesus.

Frank H Mashaw. (20th Century)

Day 28

For we must needs die,
and are as water spilt on the ground,
which cannot be gathered up again;
neither doth God respect any person: yet doth he devise
means, that his banished be not expelled from him.
2nd Samuel Ch14 v14

The Lord Jesus said:
I am come that they might have life,
and that they might have it more abundantly.
John Ch10 v10

The Lord Jesus said:
Verily, verily, I say unto you, He that heareth my word,
and believeth on him that sent me, hath everlasting life, and
shall not come into condemnation;
but is passed from death unto life.
John Ch5 v24

Jesus said unto her, I am the resurrection, and the life:
he that believeth in me,
though he were dead, yet shall he live:
And whosoever liveth and believeth in me shall never die.
John Ch11 v25-26

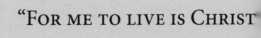

"FOR ME TO LIVE IS CHRIST

There is life for a look at the Crucified One,
There is life at this moment for thee;
Then look, sinner, look unto Him and be saved,
Unto Him who was nailed to the tree.

Oh, why was He there as the bearer of sin,
If on Jesus thy guilt was not laid?
Oh, why from His side flowed the sin-cleansing blood,
If His dying thy debt has not paid?

It is not thy tears of repentance or prayers,
But the blood that atones for the soul;
On Him, then, who shed it, thou mayest at once
Thy weight of iniquities roll.

Then take with rejoicing from Jesus at once
The life everlasting He gives;
And know with assurance thou never canst die,
Since Jesus, thy righteousness, lives.

Amelia Matilda Hull. (1825 - 1884)

.ND TO DIE IS GAIN." PHILIPPIANS
1:21

65

OUR FRIEND AND CONFIDANT

*T*here is a Friend upon whom we can all rely, no matter what our circumstances are and no matter who we are: His name is Jesus. He isn't just a very dear Friend but He is the very best of friends because of who He is and what He has done. The Bible tells us that the love He expressed toward us while we were at our worst; *"while we were yet sinners,"* is enough to prove to us that His love does not depend upon our performance, which is good news because there is *"none righteous, no, not one." (Romans Ch3 v10).*

Now, if this dearest of friends called Jesus has done all it takes to give us access into the very presence of God the Father for forgiveness and cleansing, how much more is there to be found by trusting in Him for our eternal wellbeing, starting here and now?

No matter what we have to pass through, there will never be a moment of time in which He fails to keep His promise to us that: *"I will never leave thee, nor forsake thee." (Hebrews Ch13 v5).* At the time when we most need a friend, that can sometime be the very time when we find ourselves all alone!

But be not downcast; for if and when everyone else fails, He will always be there for you.

This is the very same precious and beloved One He has always and forever been.

Nevertheless God

Down through the ages since time did first begin -
The human race
Has had its trials without and fears within, because this place
Is marred by sin and suffering day by day, but oh, His own,
His own dear ones can confidently say - they're not alone.

On every side there's trouble but we cheer -
The way is straight.
Perplexed are we but never in despair - on Him we wait.
When bearing His reproach, He's by our side,
What strength this gives.
We often are cast down but not destroyed, because He lives.

We're not exempt from suffering that is true, 'Nevertheless -
God' gives to us a reason to go through. We must confess -
When those we thought would stay did leave instead,
He's always near.
Through each temptation and each trial were led,
We need not fear.

If for "a little while" we hurt within, we'll bravely take
Our Friend that sticketh closer than our kin, He'll n'er forsake!
What hope, what wondrous hope,
From gloom to raise the soul to cheer.
The trying of our faith will bring us praise
And dry our tear.

AleB

Day 29

THE BEGINNING OF WISDOM

The fear of the LORD is the beginning of wisdom:
and the knowledge of the holy is understanding.
Proverbs Ch9 v10

And the child grew, and waxed strong in spirit, filled with
wisdom: and the grace of God was upon him.
And Jesus increased in wisdom and stature,
and in favour with God and man.
Luke Ch2 v40-52

O the depth of the riches
both of the wisdom and knowledge of God!
how unsearchable are his judgments,
and his ways past finding out!
Romans Ch11 v33

Let the word of Christ dwell in you richly in all wisdom;
teaching and admonishing one another
in psalms and hymns and spiritual songs,
singing with grace in your hearts to the Lord.
Colossians Ch3 v16

Father of light! conduct my feet
Through life's dark, dangerous road;
Let each advancing step still bring
Me nearer to my God.

Let Heav'n eyed prudence be my guide;
And when I go astray,
Recall my feet from folly's paths
To wisdom's better way.

Teach me in every various scene
To keep my end in sight;
And whilst I tread life's mazy track,
Let wisdom guide me right.

That heavenly wisdom from above
Abundantly impart;
And let it guard, and guide, and warm,
And penetrate my heart;

Till it shall lead me to Thyself,
Fountain of bliss and love;
And all my darkness be dispersed
In endless light above.

Christopher Smart. (1722 - 1771)

Day 30

Though I walk in the midst of trouble, thou wilt revive me:
thou shalt stretch forth thine hand against the wrath
of mine enemies, and thy right hand shall save me.
Psalm 138 v7

Behold, the LORD'S hand is not shortened,
that it cannot save;
neither his ear heavy, that it cannot hear:
Isaiah Ch59 v1

She shall bring forth a son,
and thou shalt call his name JESUS:
for he shall save his people from their sins.
Matthew Ch1 v21

This is a faithful saying, and worthy of all acceptation,
that Christ Jesus came into the world
to save sinners; of whom I am chief.
1st Timothy Ch1 v15

Wherefore he is able also to save them to the uttermost
that come unto God by him,
seeing he ever liveth to make intercession for them.
Hebrews Ch7 v25

I have a Redeemer who saves me from sin;
Now He's abiding forever within,
His life for my ransom so freely He gave -
'Tis Jesus my Saviour, mighty to save.

I have a Redeemer to pilot me o'er
Life's angry billows to Heaven's fair shore;
I know He will keep me, tho' wild be the wave -
'Tis Jesus my Saviour, mighty to save.

I have a Redeemer, so watchful is He,
Walking beside me, my terrors all flee;
He guards me in danger, and bids me be brave -
'Tis Jesus my Saviour, mighty to save.

I have a Redeemer, I know He is mine,
Proving His presence by power divine;
I surely can trust Him to conquer the grave -
This Jesus my Saviour, mighty to save.

Gordon Vincent Thompson. (1888 - 1965)

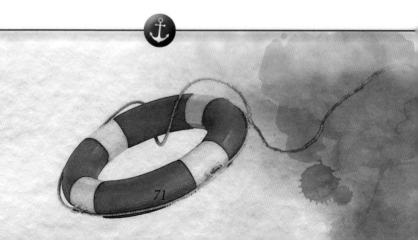

IT IS NO SECRET

*S*tuart Hamblen was a larger than life, alcohol dependent, singer, song writer, and radio personality. In 1949 through the persuasion of his wife Hamblen went to hear the young evangelist Billy Graham in Los Angeles. Here he was convicted of his sin and need for Christ. After a couple of night's struggle he phoned the evangelist in the early hours of the morning seeking peace with God. His salvation and resulting change in lifestyle was dramatic especially when a year later his radio station sacked him for refusing to run adverts from manufacturers of alcohol! Shortly after his conversion, Hamblen met John Wayne, at that time probably the most famous actor in the world. 'Say Stuart,' Wayne commented, 'I hear you've got religion?' 'Well John,' Hamblen replied truthfully 'It's no secret what God can do!' The actor paused before replying, 'That sounds like some kind of song title if you ask me.' That night Hamblen went home and wrote *It is no Secret what God can do*. And indeed it is no secret at all. The God who changed Stuart Hamblen's life and eternal destiny is still the God who saves souls, mends lives and repairs broken homes by His love and grace. If you haven't yet come to realise the seriousness of your sin or appreciate all that the Lord Jesus Christ, the Son of God, did for you when He died on the cross, why not turn from your sin now and trust Him as your Saviour. It will be a moment you will rejoice in for all eternity in Heaven.

The chimes of time ring out the news
Another day is through.
Someone slipped and fell,
Was that someone you?
You may have longed for added strength
Your courage to renew
Do not be disheartened;
For I have news for you.

It is no secret what God can do,
What He's done for others, He'll do for you.
With arms wide open, He'll pardon you,
It is no secret what God can do.

There is no night; for in His light
You never walk alone,
Always feel at home
Wherever you may roam
There is no power can conquer you
While God is on your side
Take Him at His promise,
Don't run away and hide

Carl Stuart Hamblen. (1908 - 1989)

Christ
Isaiah Ch9 v6
Isaiah Ch53 v5
Philippians Ch2 v6-8
Hebrews Ch12 v2
1st Peter Ch1 v18-19

Encouragement
Psalm 121 v1-2
Isaiah Ch40 v31
Isaiah Ch43 v2
John Ch14 v27
Romans Ch8 v31

Faith
John Ch11 v25-26
Romans Ch10 v9
2nd Corinthians Ch5 v7
Hebrews Ch11 v6
Hebrews Ch12 v2

God
Joshua Ch1 v9
Psalm 38 v8
Psalm 138 v8
Romans Ch10 v13
Romans Ch11 v33

Grace
Numbers Ch24 v24-26
Isaiah Ch30 v18
2nd Corinthians Ch12 v9
Ephesians Ch2 v8-9
Hebrews Ch4 v12

Hope
Psalm 42 v11
Jeremiah Ch29 v11
Lamentations Ch3 v24
Romans Ch15 v13
1st Peter Ch3 v15

Love
Psalm 116 v1-2
John Ch15 v13
Romans Ch8 v38-39
Ephesians Ch2 v4-5
1st John Ch4 v19

Mercy
Psalm 25 v6-7
Psalm 51 v1-2
Proverbs Ch28 v13
Isaiah Ch30 v18
Micah Ch7 v18

Peace
Psalm 4 v8
Isaiah Ch26 v3
John Ch16 v33
Romans Ch5 v1
Philippians Ch4 v6-7

Rest
Psalm 37 v7
Psalm 91 v1-2
Matthew Ch11 v28-30
Mark Ch6 v31
Hebrew Ch4 v9

Safety
Psalm 27 v1
Psalm 46 v1
Proverbs Ch18 v10
Nahum Ch1 v7
Romans Ch8 v38-39

Strength
1st Chronicles Ch16 v11
Psalm 76 v23
Isaiah Ch40 v29
2nd Corinthians Ch12 v9
Philippians Ch4 v13

Trust
Psalm 9 v10
Psalm 56 v3
Proverbs Ch29 v25
Jeremiah Ch17 v7-8
Philippians Ch4 v19

Amanda Le Bail

*A*t the age of seventeen, Amanda began a search for the truth inspired by a promise from God passed on to her four years earlier: "Ye shall seek me, and find me, when ye shall search for me with all your heart." *Jeremiah Ch29 v13.* Through reading her Bible she came to understand her need as a sinner for God's forgiveness. With the help of her Grandparents she finally came to trust in the Lord Jesus as her personal Lord and Saviour some months afterwards.

Having learned that: 'God is able' in all circumstances, Amanda seeks to represent Him as 'the Father of mercies' to poor lost sinners, and 'the God of all comfort' to His weary people.

Her Internet ministry allows her to freely express words of comfort and inspiration using her love for writing articles, poetry, music and songs etc. You can visit her website at www.restawhile.co.uk.

Robert Plant

Originally from Yorkshire Robert became a Christian through the witness of a friend at school when he was sixteen. Up until this point he had never heard the message of the Gospel. In 1993 Robert left his employment as a Safety Manager to proclaim the message of salvation through faith in the Lord Jesus Christ. He has written several books for Children along with various Gospel and Bible teaching booklets. He and his wife reside on the Antrim Coast of Northern Ireland close to the Giant's Causeway.